False-Positive:
the Quarantine Verses

geoff peterson

authorHOUSE®

AuthorHouse™
1663 Liberty Drive
Bloomington, IN 47403
www.authorhouse.com
Phone: 833-262-8899

Published by AuthorHouse 09/26/2022

ISBN: 978-1-6655-6868-5 (sc)
ISBN: 978-1-6655-6867-8 (e)

Library of Congress Control Number: 2022915257

Print information available on the last page.

Any people depicted in stock imagery provided by Getty Images are models, and such images are being used for illustrative purposes only. Certain stock imagery © Getty Images.

This book is printed on acid-free paper.

Front cover art courtesy of Jackie Goldman

The Literature of Missing Persons

previous titles by geoff Peterson

for Rufus
and Mandy-Over-the-Moon

A new age began—empty, sober, and joyless, like a sheet of white paper.

—Bruno Schulz
Sanatorium Under the Sign of the Hourglass

...it is impossible for us to be surrounded by worldly honor and at the same time to bear heavenly fruit.

—Amma Syncletica, 4th cent. A.D.

Contents

To Be Continued Unnoticed

1.

Don't blame me, it was suggested I do this—by "a licensed mental health provider," no less.

"You're depressed," he says, and suggests I take it slow. "List the things you miss so you can say goodbye." He means make some scratches on paper and maybe say something—you know, constructive.

Over the course of my life I haven't learned healthy ways of feeling alive.

"That's a start," he says. "Let's explore healthy ways to incorporate in your days going forward, shall we?"

He quotes from my file under *Neurological Disorders*. Sense jangled, sockets suctioned by quarantine, and protocols for proceeding to checkout... Shortness of breath? Easy; insert more commas.

What do I miss? I miss loitering with a waitress too broke to die. I miss holing up in a movie till closing, then coming out and wondering what happened.

Areas of competence include mimicry, an interest in the occult, theosophy, poets of dead languages... Books gulped in one sitting. Not book-learning *per se*, but...reading to *feel* something.

Coffee, cigarettes, box scores: the pleasures of mid-century. Train-waiting, dog-eared passages in potboilers off drugstore racks, dreaming of my own promise...

What do I miss, you ask?

Everything.

Everything

2.

To be loved, a blind ambition once. A lust for furtive creatures in order to fix them. Jazz in the loft, "deep shadows cut by key light," and voices wet with fog...

How can I again embody a mythic reality? I miss moments breathed deeply, without remorse or pity. I miss sleeping in cars in forbidden lots, and smoking all night at my debriefing.

Overhearing grown-ups design their lives, I miss the words neglected or thrown away. I miss having a body. I miss my brain on speed-dial: a room, a meal, a girl in transit...the words forgotten while the melodies hum themselves.

Mother heard it and tried saying it, to get me to say it, to keep talking until it came out—the wonder of it: I am the parent that made me this way. I'm talking about you now. I know who's reading this. I know who you are.

Potboiler

3.

A book dashed off by an author to keep his readership occupied while he worked on a book important to him but that would take longer to finish. A potboiler the fruit of marketing schemes designed to keep his name in the public eye.

Citing potboilers by her favorites of the period: O'Hara, Cronin, Taylor Caldwell…back when a guy's "member" was erect and "her sex" a discrete glimpse of Venus. Good reads, mostly, but not up to their standard. Writers once hailed as brilliant had either "lost their way" politically, or were brought down by society dames.

My grandmother pronounced it thus between pulls on a fresh-lit Chesterfield that lent her words a sober authority.

Question: Do writers write potboilers on purpose?

No, writers work on what they think will be a distinguished piece. But things go haywire, like most things in life. Something you think will happen, doesn't. Or the sum total of ingredients that go into the book falls flat. Or the one thing that makes it all possible fails to show. If a writer recognizes this failure early, he's lucky. If not, he will work for months to come to nothing.

Like the risk taken by falling in love, I imagined. But that would come later.

But he's signed a contract with his publisher. There's a deadline. He'll stop drinking to make last minute changes. And when his editor complains, he'll act insulted. Maybe it was the booze, or the alimony owed an ex-wife. He'll never know. But deep down he fears it's the end, that his talent has run dry, and pours another drink.

If my grandmother were here she'd note how sadly things turn. Now everything's a potboiler. Editors intent on stirring the pot for a fast buck, so that a writer never learns his limits, never sees what he can do.

Some grandmothers make it their job to suggest to a boy that the world is bigger than his parents would allow, and that its secrets need decoding. It was my grandmother who encouraged me to write my own books. She'd say go upstairs where it's quiet, and she would call me for dinner.

I'd listen to ballgames and gaze out the window. Then one day I came downstairs with a story. It was called "The Bartender" and it took place in the Big Easy. She said help yourself to the coffee cake. When she finished reading she lowered her glasses, tapped the ash on her cigarette, and said: "You know, some potboilers don't pretend to be anything else; they don't have to. I think you have something here."

Dawn Patrol

4.

I can't tell if I'm dreaming or wetting the bed.
The sleep that comes at dawn assures me I'm safe,
the night light still on.

That shaft of sun from the window—my entire span on earth,
a séance of objects and what's between them:
bed made, birds fed, plants watered...

Of not being rooted in time & place: never was or could be.
But as secret progeny of an ancient time & craft—
I stand firm.

Break 5.

Fry up a fast egg sandwich like Fast Eddie in *The Hustler*.
Rub the snot from both eyes and scroll to the page
I deleted yesterday.

Such vastness…
like running your hand over a table reserved by the hour.
A pity you have to break the racked balls to begin.

Trembling

6.

The wind hums like a crisis of the heart. My car runs but for a tire that's sluggish. The moon hangs on somewhere, empty of schemes.

Manage your decline in modest steps, says my primary care provider: one lap less in the pool and fewer trips to the grocer...

I call my friends at inconvenient times. Yoga, they say, or returning a book. They say to call back in an hour, but by then I've forgotten.

Today I'll consider the time it takes for cream to dissolve in rich black coffee. Maybe by then I'll have nodded off with the cup halfway to my lips.

The Silence

Even the music is tedious...

Cataloged recordings by artists and their flip sides with notes...
rarely played now, music of late an aberration,
and silence what is lost.

Music interprets one's solitude, while silence conducts its business
in dreams.

Played in my head with ghosts sprinting like they're not there,
musicians of old with hearts cranked on arpeggios.
So many gone...

it's strange being the one left to make the coffee.

Stir-Fry

8.

Strange, last night,
deciding what to have for dinner,
an overwhelming urge to call my father.

Every night I'd make the same thing.
We ate in silence:
chop-sticks.

Night Train

9.

It's hard anymore. You have to think ahead. Tickets, mask, money, ID, keys, notes and delays as posted. "It doesn't matter where you are, if you're waiting for a train it's always the same place."

The ruddy-cheeked barrel racer in western boots and buckskin stares blankly. It's another language to her. I'll shut up now. I don't wish to offend or be noticed by cameras.

They board me in steerage. I get the window and gaze out at lights, rolling now. Stops at Maricopa, Yuma, Indio…coast bound, not talking but thinking in the darkness between towns, thinking about my life. Not seeking solutions or replaying scenes. Just thinking.

I clock the odometer miles on my life. And songs the words keep changing to, melodies that blend with dust and create altered states and the beings that occupy them.

When it hits me: *that cowgirl in Tucson was my ex-wife, back from the dead. Bruised, puffy, and traveling with orders.*

Imagine, L.A. and I did not come to get an award, but to bond with men set among palm trees or nodding in restroom stalls. Coffee, fried chicken. Back from elsewhere in the mind, they talk with their hands, all our lives far away and floating.

Downtown couples, masked, packing babies. Old men in Dodger caps like Aztec priests. Everywhere there's a line. Joined at the end, watch the vendors at understaffed booths be feverish in their rhythms—barking, cutting, wrapping, counting money…

Walk in search of a room at the old places, firetraps mostly—since converted to lofts, condos, Section-8 listings... A man pays to keep safe. Laundered sheets, a pillow. At the Hotel Barclay I'm told it's over and done with. Heather, for one, who wrote a love note in water colors and slipped it under my door the day I left. And Hank who quoted odds makers but wouldn't bet on dogs or horses... Given notice, both. Be out and off the premises, as ordered. Both of them, fixed income, no family left.

That was the day I was done with California forever. It's been decades. I'm not really here. Friends think I am but I'm not. With no place to go, I'll repair to a place in Chinatown that charges double because I'm too early to check in on Pacific Coast Time.

I'll pay anything. Just give me what you got so I can lie down and make this go away.

It's what history has to teach us.

Los Angeles

10.

Sirens from far off hover above the night's Pacific:
screams of souls falling into awareness.

A faint whiff of the perfume of the past
splashed on to go out for the evening.

How could I know, I hadn't seen them behind their masks.
Truly, what had I done to make this my struggle?

Despite the attention and care given by others, in the end
a man goes to a room, closes the door, and sits.

I don't recall renting a room here, but promise I'll remember
next time, upon checking out.

Approaching Oscar

"I can stand anything but pain," raved Oscar Levant
in *The Band Wagon*.

Remembering the mug on that guy makes me
hug myself harder.

Nerve disorder, as diagnosed. If it fails to kill you,
it will not make you younger.

A danger to myself—not suicide, *per se*, but
harm self-inflicted.

Those who know had once lived here but
chose to resist its allure.

When life becomes a burden and you decide it's time,
says the girl: *call me first.*

The Odds

The odds of being in rm. 408 in the City of Angels are slim.

There's a bug right there. Wings, nervous feelers. He likes my title. It's in neon and lights up with letters missing. *Beelzebug,* a bar or an all-nite laundry.

There! at the edge of the page, see him? Weighing whether to crawl, jump or fly away like a bad bet. *Gambling problem?* barks the radio*, call…*

Was that the phone just now—at this hour? Calls from a *doppelgänger* hired to forward my mail. Postmark Cuzco or Malaga. Or somewhere between.

Tonight the thought of doing nothing compresses all thought into panic.

I've decided not to spend tonight here. It's not safe. I'm the only person on this floor. What are the odds of that happening? What odds do seismologists give when the ground of being is out of order?

I know this passage. I've memorized it. I will walk out before dawn and get no farther than a block where a girl, homeless, everything in a sack, waits for the light to change to cross over.

I will stop to watch her, to watch where she goes, and why.

Naked Man: a film treatment

13.

> It will not occur to me till later that I am naked, and nobody said a word.
>
> —*Alone, with groceries* (2020)

A man walks into an office naked. Enter: Naked Man. He comes in the back and proceeds to a desk marked Manager. He takes a seat. Workers are busy with phones. Few look up, no one's alarmed, at least so you'd notice. It's not the first time Naked Man's appeared in a film.

Previously the Manager was away from his desk. But today's different. It's early when he gets off the phone, looks up and sees Naked Man. "What can I do for you?"

"Hello. I've come here to look it over, and have decided I like it. I have an aunt living out on the highway and I'm staying at a motel nearby. This is a nice chair. I like a chair with arms."

A secretary drapes a blanket over the man's shoulders. Someone brings coffee. Naked Man sips, smacks his lips, sighs. It reminds him of something.

The Manager is a man in his thirties. Shaven, married, hair parted. Boyish, you'd say. He could be a pitcher whose career hinges on his luck at impressing coaches that his injuries are behind him. He recognizes that he has to keep talking to honor the dream, to keep it going and see where it leads.

Naked Man takes this all in before resuming. "You see, I know which dreams are for the living and which are from the dead. I bring a message from the future."

Naked Man rises, leans, whispers in the Manager's ear. Message delivered, the trance breaks up. Staff resumes working. Deadlines to meet. Roll opening credits…

And like all dreams it could run on and get filed in the archive. Soon we forget them. Or we jot them down and commence to blood-let. Prick their flesh, squeeze, toss in the laundry.

Now wake up. Wear the blanket back to your car and sit there. Finish your coffee. Across the street someone leaves your room at the motel. Watch now to see if it's you.

Road Rocket

14.

Frequency goes first. Untapped purée of semen. Urinary problems and getting to the toilet in time… Libido crushed by Beta-blockers. Breathless making the bed.

Two years ago I told Fred I drove thirty miles to bump into a girl named Josie—accidentally on purpose, as it were. Like a kid.

He hung up on me. One month later he was dead. I called and got a message: *Hello…you don't know me but Fred says it's no use calling.*

Metastasis. Thoracic cancer, built into the grammar, every noun, verb and participle, as diagrammed.

Asleep when you don't know it—*where have I been?* Is there a word for it? *Dementia,* says the faucet in the splash of a single drop. Now where were we?

Need a ride, young lady? California, I'll bet. Out where they make the movies. Hop in.

The Call
15.

It comes to all men, the call to come in and discuss your tests in the morning. Organs in crisis, kidney or gall bladder… A clock stammers to what's coming.

Stretch, dress, wash, brush, drops in both eyes, hearing aids, ballpoint pen and 13—count 'em— pills…keys, water, phone, money…what it takes to get out and show up smiling.

Ordered to remove clothing, you appear pale, atrophied, scrawny…

No need to decipher what they're saying. You're living it. You heard it inside you and are stunned it's real. MRI, CAT scan, biopsy. The technology tells its own story. It's the treatment that kills you.

What's left to be afraid of? Losing your last friend. Being alone. Dying alone. Blindness and wearing crumbs on your chest. Losing your mind.

When a death sentence is handed down, survivors will close ranks in a club called The Living.

Back home run the film backwards: strip down, make coffee, tune in ballgame, heat up leftovers…

Now sit back and listen to fans howling at a bad call a thousand miles away.

Mysteries

16.

Her lap is a sacrificial altar; her skin a soma press; the two lips of the vulva are the fire in the middle.
                    —Upanishads, 500 B.C.

Part of me is dead, an old man who sips his life from a saucer,
so I know what I'm missing.

Kneeling at a shrine of lost souls as before the vulva of my beloved
splayed on an unmade bed...

I would savor the scent of both and walk away refreshed.

Hanging On

New Year's in a dentist's chair, clutching my thighs... Amazing how they hang on, she says, poking my molars.

When *they* go, it's over: heart, jaw, intestines... No one returns your calls, and in case you haven't noticed: *your ass falls off!*

Consonants mangled by a steel-clawed prong. Seated in the Chair of Forgetfulness as close to God as there is. Not to worry, she says, something will get you before they abscess.

An asteroid perhaps, due at midnight. Best viewed on an empty stomach, says the TV in the ceiling. A pity you can't stay awake long enough to see it.

Tradition

18.

As reported, the wisdom of the land and the wisdom of the sea, the wisdom of land's end and the wisdom of oblivion...
(a bell sounds)

Go down to the locker of maps & model ships...inside a clock's ticking from the winter you were born.

Descend by fathoms in a bladder of old poems until hearkened by the squeal of machinery... Enter the depths, the wreck on the bottom.

Let your heart drift and be hidden from the world.

Locomotives & Cabooses

19.

Some men are locomotives, others are cabooses, the saying goes. Reading it over, it's the best I can make out:

I'm the only customer in the place when he introduces himself. He's an A-list director whose name you'd recognize, given the time and place. He's only in town for a minute, and just stopped for coffee before meeting his ride. He's scouting locations and was about to leave when he noticed what I'm reading.

"I directed that," he says, pointing to my text. "Off-Broadway, years ago."

He lists people he worked with, a Who's Who of Actor's Equity of that period. He slams a pill with coffee when I mention I too was in New York then. He looks at me strangely. "I thought you looked familiar!"

There is no reason why I should look familiar to this man. No evidence to suggest he would ever recognize me as somebody other than myself—that is, no one he'd likely meet "off-Broadway" or anywhere else.

"What were you doing then?" he asks.

"Drinking."

He breaks into a grin that could double for something else. "Of course," he says. "Off-Broadway, no doubt."

There is no reason this man should be scouting locations when people are trained to do that. Unless… the budget's tight and what you see is their latest cost-cutting measure. He launches into a synopsis of his latest project—when I'm reminded of a line from a Russian poem:

All my losses/Are here beside me.

The man seals the lid on his coffee and looks away, expecting his ride. "Well, like they say: Some men are locomotives, others...I'm sure you understand."

I offer no reply. I want him to sit with that remark on his lips for as long as the dream lasts. Time has not been kind to this man, who I swear you'd recognize, given the time and place.

Curvature

20.

Wake up, log dreams, gulp pills, scan photos of a used-up life…
It's my job: kids, dogs, pictures taken.

Come puberty the kid that's me would be sullen, failing math
and reading the wrong books…

At first you think it's the end of the world, then you think it's only
the end.

If something cannot go on forever, it will stop, said an economist.
Life goes on, but stops short.

If a friend covers great distance to see me, he'll follow the sun going down:
worth a cup of coffee.

By the time we meet the clocks have changed and we struggle knowing
where to start.

Grievance is real, we say. History embraces no right or wrong side.
Only endurance.

As for the books I keep and the injuries inscribed: scars so feeble I can't
help but love them.

Home   21.

Be in advance of all parting.
        —Rilke

Nine years ago I carried this same mattress up 14 steps to the door of our shack, dropped it, collapsed upon it and announced I'd not move again.

I must've known something. That she'd leave soon and beat a path home, leaving the mattress, a table, a lamp with no shade.

98 degrees the day we pulled up in the truck. Failure to replenish fluids enough, grizzled, sweaty, we melted by the hour.

I knew then that I'd stay for the rest of my life in a room talking to myself and waiting till dark to go out.

The night moans like a man tossing in a dream. And here I remain a witness to what's brought me here in the first place.

Horror Vacui

On bad days I can't stop having pain in the eye I see myself with. Prone to blackout, convulsions, at dawn I sit in the Chair of Forgetfulness and watch birds fidget.

The clothes in my closet haven't been worn in twenty years.
I have started on the road that leads down.

Spooked by unnamed sources I forget what I've seen. I shovel beans from a paper plate. Suddenly I clutch myself in the chair and squeeze.

A gerontologist said pain causes insomnia which induces fatigue, which leads to isolation, then depression which causes memory loss…which leads to panic.

And all that's left is you, this room, this—(?)

Party Line

23.

My neighbors are old and call each other almost every morning to ask:
"Do you have food in your house?"

If the answer's yes we hang up, confident of our rights to another twenty-four.
Then we sit at our windows, watching.

Sunset Express

24.

The photos on my wall urge me to feel the same way about the same things…

Mother, father: framed. My sisters as kids. My daughters then & now…
Abelard & Eloise at study. Mary Magdalene's selfie.
Van Gogh's chair. Clemente's rookie card.
Myself at eight.

When my friend meets with her grown children and their children,
just before they catch flights out to coastal cities
to resume careers…

she cannot contain such depth of feeling and must take a cab home
to lie down for a nap.

But first she must tell someone the astounding news of her new-found
peace, and what it might mean. I'd call it
"the sunset express," I say, for when
the heart is full and you sense the end.

She gasps, Thank you, that's it!

Call me later when you wake up.

Hours pass. I would call her to check but I already know better.
There will be no answer. Ringing, no answer, over & over.
There will be no answer.

I'm gazing at the pictures on my wall while imagining an answer.

Dream Trope

25.

Besides waking to pee, the only thing that gets me to roll over
and switch on a light: the urge to jot it down in a notebook
on the page marked with a holy card of Pancho Villa.
On the back it reads, God bless Chata, Lucero…
and our cousins in Culiacán.

Pharmacopeia

26.

All my meds are named so that I can't pronounce them. At six I roll over and pop a 50 mg. Levothyroxine for "thyroid replacement."

At seven I make a breakfast of two Valsartan (320 mg.), Metoprolol Tartrate (25 mg.), and Hydrochlorothiazide (a 12.5 mg. cap)—gulped with Metamusil.

At seven I can't find my mouth with my hands, never mind polysyllabic fats. Barely able to record dreams in sentences before they cool.

At night it's Metoprolol redux (25 mg.) and Pravastatin (20 mg.) for cholesterol, + a shiny 300 mg. Gabapentin for "chronic pain."

Pain-killers lose effectiveness, said a neurologist upping my dosage. He prescribes for me but it's a race against time. At the end I'll request morphine and cozy up to the Big Sleep.

Nickolai my neighbor flushed his meds in his 76th year. Solitude, pills, a studio with an emergency button by the toilet: he saw where it was headed.

For five days he lay with his hands clamped to a cup of coffee. And to think a week earlier he was getting a blow-job from a girlfriend in a barber's chair after closing.

Meet Rufus

27.

The best I can figure it, everyone's from somewhere else. Friends waiting tables, the figure M in her personhood... Corn Belt, Rust Belt, down & dirty.

Even Rufus, brought to the hospital by an aunt after my surgery. Rufus who waits for me and hollers, "When you coming to bed?"

Illinois born & bred, back before the trees were cut and he feasted on muskrat and grubs...

Abandoned early, soon adopted by a family heading west. Three kids, a dog. Rufus smothered by the mother's rambunctious affection.

After the parents divorced, dropped at a 2nd hand shop in a baby stroller. Look at him, said my aunt, fresh from the same store-wide sale, *isn't he adorable?*

I told a friend that Rufus is no ordinary bear, and shared a photo of him peeking out from the covers. She thought I said Refuse, and warned me against lice.

I did not feel the need to correct her.

Love Has Stranded Me

My past life seeks the next bright thing to keep me attentive…
turning over cards from the Tarot and sleeping on a friend's floor,
upstairs, under a light bulb, the window cracked to let
ballgames in—fathers & sons, bats & balls,
and the wives holding the beer.

Again years later, back in the town she once escaped to,
not to win back her old job, but to freelance.
I thought she understood what it meant
to stay *out there, somewhere other*…
past lives the map to one's heart.

Time's Up

Something for pain. Like a homeless guest mumbling between mouthfuls: *What else you got?*

Will someone tell the pain there's nothing in the cupboard, *check for yourself.* Don't laugh, it only makes you cough.

How the hours grind their teeth and yawn. Let death meet me on a fog-lit corner, I pray. Set the timer.

Alone in bed one hand squeezes the other.

No one to call, to come take charge...take my pulse, touch my brow...*hmm, what have we here?*

Bad dreams and holy cards. Feel it. Bless the pain so you may be strengthened. There will be no rest, no sleep, no waking to a new day. That's hell, isn't it, being with no place to be?

So be it.

Birthday Boy

30.

I wake up no longer supported by this life.
Living it, the act of it, diaphanous, imponderable,
persists with or without me.

Having cruised the song cycles of Brahms, Mahler…
I can't help but hanker for Cowboy Otis's range ballads,
or the Drifting Sons of Heaven.

Again I am ten years old and promised a pony.
Forgive my rudeness, my dear uncles and aunts,
but I can't ride with you watching.

One Good Line

31.

To jot a good line on the palm of my hand
to better remember it,

only to lose it when Rufus licks my palm...
is what happens when you die.

Senior Residence

The maintenance guy fixes my faucet and says it's simple really, no reason I can't do it myself. He doesn't need to remind me the place is decrepit with oozing sores. Moldy floors, cracks in the plumbing, the refrigerator's death rattle...

I don't know how to tell him that I can't see close up. But that's not it. It is but there's more. And that's what I have a hard time with. I want to say he has no idea what an achievement it was to bring myself to call him, but I don't. He wouldn't understand. I thank him for coming and tip him hugely.

Altar Boy

Adjust the scented cruet bought 2nd hand,
and the spray flasks on hand-me-down saucers
arranged tastefully before the mirror...

Add a vase of paper flowers to be dusted
and put back smartly.

You see, any artist worth his calling
must attend to a fetish.

Approaching False-Positive 34.

A quarantine not COVID inflected but of my own free will,
being ordered to work my voices.

I choose January to deep dive and drift with currents…
for the benefit of souls and the refreshment of a world that was.

January when those I love choose to die and end their grievance,
and nothing's left but drafty rooms and a radio.

How to proceed inside the cloud of unknowing in desperate times?
Write the book.

Get your tattered house in order, they urge. Or better yet,
burn it down.

Nocturne

These solemn winter nights, after supper and the bowl put away,
I retire to the Chair of Forgetfulness
in the pure dark and count
backwards…

I cannot tell if my eyes are open or shut, or if it's you or her
or someone coming with a message…
Or merely the dark being itself.

Workshop 36.

An artist advised me: when you complete a project, start something right away. Artists between works are nervous, fretful, and deranged with regret.

Art is more than entering a room and throwing paint on canvas. But life itself. Belong to it or don't bother coming back.

Last Stop

I would sell my shack and head north to look around.
A town in Nevada with a cafe called Curly Horse,
a Keystone filling station with crank pumps...
street signs with the names worn smooth,
and a hotel left over from the boom.
Rent me a suite with a brass bed,
a bowl & pitcher and a window
whose curtain billows...
And a train way off.

Drifting Off While Watching a Western

38.

The last thing a man notices in this his final scene
after taking a bullet in his chest:

The earth is bounded
and the sky without limit.
All there is surrounds
and runs through us
without end.

Losing It

Today I forgot how to spell *maybe*. I wrote *mabe*—didn't look right.
Then *mabey*. Close, but no cigar.

In the dictionary I forgot D comes after C.
So: *decline...defogger...dementia…*
Stop right there.

I texted my daughter, a doctor who said see a doctor—
at once, not tomorrow.

There are lower gears driving my life as I know it:
there's sitting hunched at my desk,
and consulting my watch.

Will do, I said.

Give Us This Day

40.

Buy it, clean it, cook it, pray over it, eat it, savor its colors and textures, mindful of each grain and fiber of legume—grown separately on farms far apart and set before you this day in a steamy sauce...

Thankful for the nourishment and for the hand trembling to my lips. And for the hearing aid that whistles with daily broadcasts from flying objects.

End-Times

I write about things seen along the rails from a moving train or a path leading to a bolted door…when the earth shakes and gathers like a rug shuffled into waves and everything woven into it breaks up and crumbles into clouds of ash.

That's how it feels since the days of my treatment for nerves as a chronic disorder, or at least a full-blown something.

But that comes later when I fall or slip climbing stairs, and all the people who would rush to help me have perished.

New Year's Eve

42.

Watching Glen and Rita work out in *Gilda* on the movie channel—
waiting for it, the line:

I hate you so much that I think I'm gonna die from it—said leaning into him,
Johnny, whom she'd crush like a Lucky Strike.
Goddammit, Ben Hecht could write.

How the words reach out from everything before and announce what drives
her: lust and its sacred rites in dinner jackets and strapless gowns…

I'd go to bed now but the neighbors' fireworks make Rufus nervous.
It's either fireworks or there's a civil war just breaking.
Mute the chatter and let *Gilda* put us to sleep.

Rufus Speaks

43.

It wasn't till day two that I began to talk to him.
A week later he replied.

He said he identified as non-binary and asked
that I call him "the."

Dear Abby, as I'm unpracticed at these things,
do set me straight:

should Rufus continue being my bunk mate,
or better we sleep apart? Please advise.

Rufus is sick

Sometimes he's dying and fed through a straw. The way he lies with covers piled just shy of his snout, staring with a dazed look that says the truth is coming. I pat his head with a warm cloth and ask what can I get him.

Get me through this, he says.

I can't tell you how much good it does me to care for him and take heart in his struggle. My therapist says bring him in, but I can't do that to the little fella. Rufus is me, and his life not something to be fucked with.

Starting Over

45.

Here it comes, the latest doubts and orbits of lunacy…
my broken book a way of curling in bed.

Failing at the art of living, I consider this rabid script
my ticket to a fresh start.

I recall squeezing a doctor's hand when introduced
in the dark of my hospital suite…

Merely the hush of her voice told me what was wrong,
and I knew I'd cross a bridge.

The bridge is your friend, she said, but you won't
know that till later.

Kindschaft 46.

Since coming to the desert I glimpse more childhood scenes than if I were back walking its leafy streets. Scenes slowed to a crawl to heighten a sense of color, composition, while the mystery unfolds.

A kindergarten of shadows pierced by sunlight. A boy's secret terror in the face of "progress," its cost in lives in spite of clunky spacemen with decoder rings...

My dead grandfather, grandmother, parents, siblings, uncles, aunts who loved me: in my heart I am there, bowing at the altar of a mumbled sacrifice...

Or trembling to kneel in the last row, behind the few faithful at a morning mass, hoping not to be noticed.

Bidding

47.

Anyone can be bought. Each of us on a daily basis by a boss, spouse or dealers in futures... A life bought and paid for, the Christian coda.

Born an instrument of a woman's bidding, I failed to get a grip on my object of worship.

A friend suggests devotion to the Mother of Sorrows, and a plea for mercy in the dark. The least visible the prayer the more enthralling to Our Lady, as cited elsewhere.

Anything to extinguish the clamor of big ideas.

Like a Russian

48.

...there was a gloom, silence and abandon that spelled revolution, disorder, economic disaster.

—Chicago Daily News, 1905

I regret not having studied the language, esp. the poems of Ahkmatova, Tsvetaeva, Blok—each in translation. Men and women in locked rooms in white-out winters, scoured of slogans and hopes for a greener world…

Pasternak's Zhivago by candlelight in his deserted home… *Nobody loves poetry like a Russian,* said Yevgraf the half-brother at a point where moonlight ices over. I wrote a friend that when we write it means a full moon. Yes, he replied, words claw their way home and delight in a lamp being lit.

Invisible Persons

49.

My uncle would take me to movies, the forbidden ones, without parental consent. Adult themes, they warned, and flesh too shiny for a boy of eight. I loved the films and especially those invited to tempt me. Uncle, are you there? Speak to me.

I advise a friend that when reminded of someone from her past, someone loved but who had since departed, to speak to them and let your hearts entwine, a most welcome prayer. And if she's devout in its practice she will see what it is about her that they loved, and perhaps she too will come to love that part of herself. That, to be sure, would make everyone happy.

Lear
50.

The final scene when he longs to join Cordelia, father and daughter, where they'd wake each day and talk over coffee about who's first, who's last, and who the up & comer... I don't have the text before me, and lives have passed since seeing it with my father and posting a review for the hometown paper.

But to make the point I was too callow to make then...*[alarum: flourish of trumpets]:* Everything's a distraction. Call it what you want, it remains unnameable.

Those who merely regard Lear a humbled monarch, stripped of honor and reduced to the howling of beasts on stormy nights, as a tragic figure—they have been fooled. Lear is a monument to a man entering his truth by paying the unthinkable. Call it the cost of doing business. The prize, at the end, is to be emptied of the charms that attach us to this world.

Remember that while watching this year's Academy Awards.

Jan. 10

Bear Dreams

51.

You grab at anything—from a bloody carcass to passages in books to who knows who rants through the wire between worlds?

And now, locked in the minutes between 8 & 10, the arms shriveled, feeling abandons the fingers, and food requires untried spices to delight the tongue.

Winter's gloom, deep for sleeping. Musing about campaigns attended, the women that exist only in the mind...and a loving glimpse of yourself, a boy in an old man's haircut...

Somewhere a fire dies, somewhere a wolf, a wind picks up and moans among the ruins, and the snakes lay coiled underground.

Phone Booth

52.

Dying is central to the experience. In a phone booth lost in time, an assassin fans the directory's pages, runs his finger down a column inch: stops at you. In the end it is what distinguishes us.

In the news kids on campus clamor for a "safe space." Make mine Nevada or Wyoming, curled in my car in a dust storm...

We are raised not to know it, nor to believe in it, but by safe space do we not mean the grave, and that we yearn to crawl down into it?

Don't get me wrong, I'm overwhelmed by phone calls. I'm still the kid who stays in his room and roams an inner geography, thus avoiding entanglements.

But today I'm at that point in the life of every room ever inhabited: the panic of all men alone with nowhere to go.

Point Omega 53.

Looking for light bulbs at a Dollar Store when what's this: in hardback for a dollar.

Author Don DeLillo will appear at noon to sign autographs! I can see it now. The line forms at Vitamins and stretches back to Light Bulbs & Batteries. *Please have your copy ready.* Like the time I'd published a novel and invited to sign copies at Ernie's Feed & Tack.

Point Omega opened a door and kept me on a course made steady. Assessing it as a unit of merchandise stamped with a price the market would bear… while engaging the work on the author's terms—and the impact it's had on me—surely worth a buck.

Being With M

We came west when I found the shack and lived on lunar time. We were in love but it didn't keep doubts from festering. By then our love was a map of occupied territory. Call it original sin. *The Human Stain*, Roth called it.

We never argued, so there was much to say. We'd wake to light swelling in the window that coated surfaces like the flesh of unnamed creatures. Some days we were the same person. But no one's more damaged than a man who doesn't know what he wants—in bed with a woman who think she does.

I told her I was a bad party guest, that I took my love straight and doomed to failure. After five months she packed everything she could bend, fold or mutilate. She'd had a dream, and love wasn't enough. But we're different, I said. We belonged one inside the other like Russian dolls. Why is that never enough?

Now there's a hole where she used to be. It shimmers then fades depending on the moon and time of day.

I keep going over it and it comes out the same. I'd never known a woman who relished so much being glum. Except my mother, her moods pacing our rooms like a diver in steel shoes... If it stayed that way the light would shatter. That's what my father felt. What he went to work to get away from.

M was an envoy from that spirit world owned and operated by my mother, or her mother, or the one before everything. That's the story I was busy living then. I had entered a chapter in the saga where certain miseries blend with sunsets.

M reported a nerve disorder that rhymes with *cthonic*, that is, bits of business in the margins of thought. Interfaced with mine, it made sense of my journey unfolding as it had. See *Underworld, Inferno*...where one wandering soul bumps into a neighbor: *What're* you *lookin' at?*

Finally I chose not to indulge the myth and thus save myself. Separated by three thousand miles and a change of underwear, we each sought an emptiness apart. Then one day in traffic I caught sight of myself in another place—*I had survived.* It took a friend to convince me that I was not interested in a living, breathing person. And that I had always been under sail on my voyage elsewhere.

Ever since she left I've been good for nothing.

8:08

55.

Strange, in the gray light Rufus stares up from the covers. I rest my eyes for ten minutes, twenty…

By 8:03 I'm in Beckett's Paris apartment: bed, table, bicycle against a wall, the dust bin from *Endgame* in the courtyard… Samuel Beckett, my first to copy. Eighteen, off to college to seek clues in the city of *isolatos*.

When they open the first thing my eyes see: 8:08 by the clock. And now, scribbling words to make sense of the usual things: 8:19.

This is what it's like to write your life away.

8:26, Jan. 17

Workshop 2

All of us who knew each other, drank beer, shared dope and our troubles with girlfriends. We wrote daily and brought it to read and jot suggestions while the others stared through smoke-rings...

There you go getting existential, they'd say. Meaning a dereliction of duty to the story and my need to remind readers that someone's in a room writing this. The poetics of puncture, they called it, referring to my habit of stabbing a passage to deflate the illusion. We were discussing a piece where I'd maintained my presence by stopping to announce, *this is not a poem*.

They loved me for it but suspected it would hurt me later. Haunt me, they said, like it were the faintest of tumors that would appear later and I'd be left jotting *haiku* blindly with the wrong end of a pen.

We already suspected it was this or the life of our fathers.

Workshop 3

57.

Too many words.
    —Ben Johnson, actor

More often it feels like hanging in the air, performing motions: opening mail, defrosting meals, paying bills, mantras yes please/no thank you...

Writing's my only prayer confident of being heard. At its center I'll stop and see myself while the words sputter and go out.

"*Workshop* is the kind of book written by someone who's tired," wrote a reviewer. "Tired of living or tired of the same delusions, only he can decide."

He points to my scant readership and dismisses us as cranks from a dark age, camped in cars and waiting for "visitors from above."

One critic said I should've heeded the voice that foresaw my wreck in wrong-way traffic and yelled *turn back!*

I wake each day and change one word I wrote yesterday. Tomorrow, wake, read over the work from yesterday, *and change the same word back*!
    —poet Jim McAuley quoting somebody.

Art requires that we not choose the easy way, he said. That we not settle for cleverness, but pronounce our exile from God and ourselves. Like desert monks, that we write for the dead. It is with the dead we cast our lot.

Workshop 4

58.

Was being born having to be enlisting in a destiny?
—Sam Shepard

Everyone's got a long-story. Mine's been diced and sprinkled on poems. My nerves do not permit me the long form except in rare circumstances called bursts.

I wrote something called "The Poet's Game." Goes like this:

I'm sorry to reply so late to your curious text/Anymore I am slow to return serves at the net/Or from the foul line...

Last year I lost thirty consecutive matches to a vixen in Spandex/Before admitting she's the one for me!

I am what I am, said the maniac-sage.

Poets' Hall

I told them I don't write poems, but books seeking the end.
And in the rear-view mirror a country of drive-ins
and roadhouses of the Pecos.

It was the last time I'd see them.
Some wouldn't return from the war in their heads.
Others poisoned by lovers, or led away in cuffs…

Shaggy headed poets with holes in their jeans,
laughing, clapping, clapping and whistling,
and waiting their turn to be heard.

Necrology

60.

Having served my time in the pursuit of it, I will enter its hallowed halls to fetch the strays. In my youth escorting their corpses to the morgue, I studied the remains...male, female, young, old...and observed the poignancy of their sex.

Many of the dead don't know they are, and it frightens me. Dead people in customary costumes, laughing…

Is not hell the body-self that clings to the cadaver after its lips are sealed? Under the gaze of a surgical lamp it haunts me.

Face to Face

61.

Groping in the dark, I found switches that didn't work. A young woman appeared and held the door ajar. I told her I am not lurking but am trying not to fall. She mumbled something and left. I can't decide whether to exit or remain in place. Maybe I've come here to escape something. I need light to use the toilet, but the toilet's a mystery as much as my being here. Suddenly I'm at a point in my life that makes no sense.

Meaning that upon waking I will know what it is to have no future, so that everything I do, say, feel—is for the last time.

Meaning at any moment I'll stop and look around… *Is that you*, the door again.

It gets interesting.

Workshop 5

62.

Learning any skill, of course, entails a certain amount of trouble.
—Gregory Mayers
Listen to the Desert

Many discover their talent early: nurse it, pursue it, but become stymied. Distracted, misdirected, or more likely crushed by disappointment, one never fully recovers.

Even should they commit to their art, their reliance upon it is strained and subject to easy dismissal. It often follows that these artists are those whose finished works are a curse.

Speak, I am listening... 63.

Who is it I must return to when my object of desire fails me,
and loneliness yawns wider than before?

You know I'm slow to act, and I refrain from keeping appointments
but the most dire.

How many have I canceled at the last minute? Don't remind me.
But show me how every lost chance leads back to you.

Ghost Riders

64.

Driving to Sonoita on a cloud-driven day and singing along to Gene Autry...
Not once getting out of the car. Cold, rainy, the bones don't forget.

I kept punching "Ghost Riders in the Sky" on the box to get the words right:
An old cowpoke went riding out one dark and windy day…

He's an old man who goes for a ride and sees a ghost herd and cowboys who
tell him shape up or chase yer ass forever.

And by the time it ends I've experienced a crisis of conscience: *Then cowboy
change your ways today or with us you will ride/Trying to catch the devil's herd
across these endless skies...*

Yippie-yi-yay, Yippie-yi-o…

I even took a turn: "Just left to get some whiskey but changed my mind
instead/and I'm heading south to watch the clouds and get my belly fed."

"Ghost Riders" on my grandpa's Victrola—over & over till the scratches
crackled and I sat on it. It took my uncle till his fiftieth birthday to get over
it. By then I'd found the tape in a discount bin:

Happy Birthday, Charley.

And in the space of thirty seconds, fifty years disappeared.

Breakfast at Joe's

65.

On my day to get groceries I stop at Joe's for breakfast and a look at the morning paper. [caution: bring your own coffee].

A cold day in January: eggs easy, steak rare, home fries with red skin, corn tortillas, ketchup and a side of cottage cheese. Got it?

This will require a massive infusion of protein and 4% fat just to get this done. It takes twelve minutes to get my food, five to wolf it down.

The woman across from me is a silver-coiffed artist who speaks high-precision Spanish. I'm nearly the age she was when she stepped away from a painting and hocked her easel. I can better understand her now, and that's what I come to tell her. "I'm sorry I ever judged you. Your work is more real than I can say."

She commutes from Nogales and has exhibited work that now leans against the walls of her *casita*. Recently I marveled at a whimsical piece from her Covid period. Currently she arranges precious stones in her studio and permits me to see her eyes glitter.

I'm cutting meat while telling my plans for when the words stop and I shut it down, the writing I mean. "I want to get a parrot, even if it costs a thousand dollars. And I'll teach it to say the most forbidden things." Next I produce an egg-shaped stone found while hiking. The plan is to inscribe poems on it from a Taoist calendar.

I'm talking like this when a naked man in a Covid mask pulls up at a table and waves to get some service. *I know this man.* Double amputee, Vietnam. On location.

The Señora lights a cigarette though it's forbidden, and without missing a beat asks me what I'm thinking.

I'm thinking how great it is not to feel envious of the brave. I tell her that and she smiles. "You must put that in your book," she says.

"I already have," I tell her, getting the check.

Book of the Vampires

66.

from *Nosferatu*

I've waited till we were alone to say this. You understand I am speaking as one learning to die. My silence broken only by newscasts in the dark. Perhaps the time is right to tell you.

I suspect you will wish to withdraw your business with me when I tell you what I know. I understand too well. I have a history of loss I will not bore you with, except to say...

I lost the love of my life as a result of a national election. Vendettas and lost chances aflame in both eyes. Being old is no excuse.

Accounts of suicides and rats gnawing on fingers: *The Book of the Vampires* in Marxist translation. Casual encounters like gunfights. Friends hunted in the cracks...rioters & *refusniks*. Passive aggression passing for an end to violence. Mutants hiding in locked phones, uncertain of everything, urged to play along, get in line. Follow the money. They have special methods for settling old scores.

"The quest for purity—moral, philosophical, political—a precondition of madness." I said, guilty as charged. The vanity of uttering the unspeakable— for that alone I stand before you, an enemy of the people.

I've misplaced my numbers for dead souls. I recall their faces, they are the same face, a man or woman laughing with gap teeth and a mole...

Testing 1-2-3: false-positive. Come back tomorrow.

I'm just looking to get out of this without further trouble. In Strauss' *Ariadne auf Naxos*, the diva greets Bacchus on the shore: *Is it you who will release me from the burden of life?*

It hurts to swallow. Isn't that an early sign of plague?

Late Chan: The Scarlet Clue (1945)

67.

5 minutes into it, Charlie Chan destroys evidence by snatching a cigarette butt from the floor of the crime scene...

If Chan is way ahead of the law in getting down to cases, then the cops are especially goofy. All their thinking is rigid, obvious and scripted by protocol. The cops are meant as a stand-in for the audience of that time.

The scene with the black chauffeur, Mr. Birmingham Brown, and Chan's #3 son, Tommy, is a set piece of racial caricature, played for laughs.

Chan hits on the white chicks. "Permit me to introduce myself," he says to Helen, an actress. (I'll maybe start the book with it, with a photo of an old guy bowing from the waist: *Permit me...* I think I'll get a hat. White, wide brimmed).

At 10 minutes it's clear the murderer is the slimy one. Clean nails, a tailored suit and correct English usage, he's a cinch. He's an executive at Cosmo Radio Center housed in a high rise with a caste system that includes a cleaning lady, technicians, actors with speaking parts and the kahuna at the top. The nearer to the top you get, the more cooperative with police they become. That's the trail of corruption, and Inspector Chan knows this.

Panicked, the murder suspect calls his boss and pleads, "What do I do?" He doesn't have to wait for an answer. The words come punched in teletype on the machine. It says to lay low and do what she tells you. Cut to the woman in a big hat, she's in on it. The woman might just be a man.

Meanwhile #3 son hangs with the black guys in the garage, baffled by their jive and getting played tricks on. But have no fear: his father, the honorable Chan, is upstairs processing clues with Confucian precision.

Oh yes, the reliable electrode gun in the building's government laboratory has a security issue. Flash Gordon, maybe—with race and laughs added. The chauffeur spooks himself by pushing a button. You root for him not to touch anything. *Don't do it!*

Upstairs, shadows of blinds on an office wall—grafted from *film noir* on the lot next door. The actress on the radio is offered a poison cigarette. One puff, she's dead. Now I get it, the reason for Chan's pilfering the cigarette in scene 1.

A man in a suit sits on a desk tossing playing cards into a fedora. Phone rings: "Hello, who's calling?" I love that. The whole movie worth this scene alone.

Everyone snoops, overhearing phone calls, whispered confessions in elevators... secret passages with doors that slide closed. Buttons and levers, rooms filling with snow: a claustrophobia of special effects. Chan unperturbed, says "Someone would have us believe dead man fall eight stories up."

The case will not be solved without the aid of a scientific gadget, something that can reach into top secret chambers. This film is really about the new kinds of crime enabled by technology. *Nobody is safe!* Chan says, "You mean to say elevator floor fell away?"

Sidebar: At the time of the film's release, Army and Marines were scorching Japanese holdouts with flamethrowers. And a dress rehearsal for the A-bomb was staged in Alamogordo.

Ten minutes, maybe fifteen, hardly a quarter of the film's running time... Anything longer a man nods off. I must've nodded off. Anyway, you get the picture.

MONOGRAM PICTURES
THE END

Metaverse

68.

My friends send me books as gifts. They mean well. Subjects I once read about leave me cold. But then I find this:

Astrophysicists in the Outback report a strange "radio transient" sending off bursts of energy in the cosmos every twenty minutes before disappearing.

I've always been dazzled by void, emptiness, absence. Outer space is cold. I am cold. Maybe I should worry. But I don't. When I tell people I've left this world and have boarded an *anti-verse* to stream backwards in time, they become alarmed. Old guys check out every minute, while others follow their phones into the jaws of the *metaverse* and live happily ever after.

De-Friended

I do not exist on social media; therefore, I do not exist,
said Descartes. Or was it Democritus?

Absence of desire, appetites keen enough to be illegal,
snipped by lobotomy...

Squatters leave deposits for tourists to ignore
at their peril—a tough dirty job

assigned to those who think they're invisible.
Maybe they are and words are tablets for the unwary.

I don't know where I'm going with this—
say anything and you're detained for questioning.

Paid in Full

70.

Only the dead have seen the end of war.
    —Mother of a Ukrainian Lieutenant, KIA

What do old men desire more than to give their lives in action? In real war, war to the death, not an exercise or an occupation that lasts forever.

But a fight to the finish.

We beseech you to invite us to your war to get our ticket punched. As men who never knew combat—the kind they talk about—we lived our middle years in comfort, softened by access, scandal, gossip…

Rescue us from infirmity, dementia, ennui… Alone and bitter, with nothing to offer but to not get in the way, we seek to fight beside those younger who have much to teach about being useful under fire…

and thereby close our accounts in arrears.

Notice of Water Shut-off

The water will be shut off to your building on Feb. 1 from 9 to 4 p.m. so that a work crew can complete necessary plumbing repairs to your unit. Upon completion of the work the water in your building will be restored. We are sorry for any inconvenience this may cause.

Taped to my door when I got home from doing laundry. I'm hardly ever not home. I write, I swim, I eat leftovers. Today's alert strikes panic: *What day is Feb. 1? Is February far away or close up? What day is today? What is today? Is this today?*

Ontological concerns—ongoing, especially in a drought, each day a step toward cremation. The politics of water and mass migrations that rely on replenishment. In what year will the parched cities empty and the cars stream north like schools of fish?

I told M it's the pool. I need it to stay alive, to move arms & legs and channel my breath in rows. To step from the pool assured of myself on a fixed income.

Life is free only in relation to what's left. It grips me with the abruptness of late news. Loss and restoration, the stream constant: water, light, the passage of souls…

Then the phone rings and shows a number that means nothing. It leaves a message. Call us, it says. It's important you call. And waiting for me in the box is mail marked *time sensitive…*

Senior Bowling

72.

I watch because it reminds me of my grandfather getting to Vegas at midnight for a cheap room and coffee grounds in packets...

The man's dead now, Vegas a necropolis, but I'll watch it and sit on the bed before a rabbit-eared console with four channels in black & white.

I'll count my winnings and fold them in my pocket, like the man's wallet that kept snapshots of kids and a girl who died by stepping into traffic.

Workshop 6

73.

Enter now the monks trailing their chants to sweeten my sleep
before dawn…

Forged in silence, I promise to copy the Latin in notebooks.

But instead will toss in a troubled sea, and by morning forget
what's been given to serve in the custody of this life.

Frailty disqualifies me as a watcher of words and those who sing them.
Words fade, says the Vulgate, and their meanings flip.

So goes the work in times of chaos.

Rufus Nervosa

74.

You know how it feels to wake up dazed, stiff and wobbly, to stumble to the toilet and stand there, waiting. That's me all day.

This morning I noticed my pancakes missing. They were right there! *Rufus, look at me, was it you?* I didn't scold him exactly.

Rufus, wake up! Can you hear me? Say something. Maybe he ate the pancakes because he cared about my diet, about my blood sugar, about *me*.

When I die let them remember I was a reader to a blind bear, starter of fires in people's hearts, as well as their cars—to save the battery while their owners roamed the sky.

Feb. 1
lunar new year

Eulogy

75.

Day by day we fell deeper into that dangerous state, a sure sign of the end, in which one feels detached from everything that is taking place outside one.
                    —Eugenia Semyonovna Ginzburg

My friend Fran Kraylik died yesterday. He was 78 and drove a '66 Mustang right up till the end. He lived alone after thirty-four years married, and enjoyed dining on Happy Meals from the drive-thru on warm days…
A veteran of the Vietnam War, Fran became a "finisher" for local union bosses, and later was instrumental in the recently disputed mayoral election. He liked watching re-runs of black & white shows from the early period: Groucho, George & Gracie, Sid Caesar, even Gayle Storm on rainy days. Fran had a gentle sense of humor and looked forward to sitting in a favorite chair with his cat Marvin and listening to the news from Slovenia. He left no survivors.

Why am I telling this? The more written the more real it becomes, is that it? I'm telling it because it doesn't make the least bit of difference to you. Because *you didn't know the man.* Even the places he would frequent have been demolished, and no one's left to take his car.

And what's the difference anyway? Why does it matter? Is the case of Fran Kraylik real or is it that each of us wants nothing so much than to matter? That it signifies the mark we leave on others—even a scar. The chance of baseball this year remains slim. Biden and Putin resume barking through channels. And when I finish this I'll go to bed and wait for sleep to absolve me of my sins.

2nd Thoughts

76.

You haven't found it yet—what you meant to say when you started.
Same old fireworks, but without light.

I know each book declares its jurisdiction, and can only come about by
making a fool of itself if need be. I understand that. But...
there are problems.

Delete the longer sketches. Delete Rufus, he adds nothing but a gnawing sense
of cuteness that of late infects everything you do.
I'm sorry that he dies; make it sooner.

And for God's sake cut the politics at the end. Talk politics and you send
the wrong message. War depends upon a dialectic of humors,
and you're no good at it.

How do you expect to get by with this—book that's not a book? A book
at war with itself. Don't do this, I urge you.

You don't have to go through with it. You haven't come all this way to write
another wayward book. Just remember I told you.

Why I've Done Nothing With My Writing

77.

...our faithfulness to a small task is the most healing response to the illnesses of our time.

—Henri J.M. Nouwen

What is it about living it that satisfies? Waking to write and the words flow forth, filling rooms like fury. Unable to brush teeth or tie shoes without phrases percolating. In traffic scribbling at stops, words so concussive nothing gets done and nowhere got to.

No cameras, no mics, no advance copies… Just a man turning back. Is the book any good, you ask? In whose power is it to answer that? It's hard to keep a grip on my own life, let alone the words flowing beneath.

The whole idea of a book with the conceit of a self-contained world, including times, place, and characters worth a damn, a world that a reader might confuse with life…is no longer possible.
—cited in a notebook

Every book a prayer, and every prayer is broken. Language is broken. Only by typing in the dark when you can't see, it gets good.

Suicide Watch

78.

My friend, a therapist, says his clients are doing well but that, having lost his love of forty years, his own grief is bottomless. I confess I'm not qualified to judge or to trust what comes out of my mouth. With nagging pain aforethought, I'm fresh out of reasonable.

We admire those who succeed at turning the page after great suffering. Read spiritual books, they say. Exercise. Meditate. Go on retreat. Make new friends. Eco-tourism, the shaman's root.

But what they omit are their basement addictions and cut rate debaucheries, subscriptions to porn sites, necromancer cults and junk bondsmen...slave junkets to Thailand, a 2nd family in Jakarta... Everybody cheats: you, me— every life has a flip side. We crave relief in secret and pretend otherwise. Besides, what's more annoying than personalities building a brand? Narcissus *go bragh*!

Look around you. Look at yourself. What do you see? We're all on suicide watch. Each of us as deranged as the late-breaking news. "Nightmares, hallucinations, and the convulsions [of] a final global dementia," as prophesied.

Quarantine's the last outpost, the elixir not counted in milligrams and boosted on TV.

I urge him to throw himself into his work and write a book called *When Your Clients Are Doing Better Than You*. "That's good," he laughs, "I like that."

Hell, I'd even buy it.

Beads

I call my sister to ask for the five sets of mysteries that
separate the decades. It's been a while.

I'm eager to get the names as they might come in handy
at the end.

She thinks maybe I'm ready to say the rosary as a return
to a faith in earnest.

And who knows? At the end our father, confined to a chair
in his nineties, took up his beads in silence.

And our uncle, years before his death, carried the rosary
everywhere, and whispered it during mass.

Saying the rosary feels like marching down a flight of stairs
to the bottom, then starting over.

Effective when enduring acute pain or panic or interminable
waits at the clinic.

Not to mention the agony at the end.

Postcard (6" x 9") 80.

I'm living at a motel till the money runs out. I told your sister I take my pills
and go for walks before the heat cranks up. I don't see a doctor but a van takes
me to the VA if I need it. Some days at the casino I get coffee at the sportsbook
where I catch the scores & highlights of the late games. In the afternoon I nap
by a fountain splashing on huge boulders that glisten of another era when I
was someone else. It's okay being old and logy when no one remembers you
from before. I'm fine being invisible. I remember walking in the desert. I asked
my ride to drop me. This will do, I said, and tipped him big. When he drove
off I dug a hole with a knife and spoon then set the box containing Rufus
in the earth. Finally I felt something—like a huge claustrophobia that had
pressed upon me all my life. And just then, it lifted. And if you think that's
a sad note to end on, then you don't know me at all.

Acknowledgments

I wish to thank Tom Burke for reminding me that Taylor Caldwell once graced this earth and wrote in earnest. And to his sister Mary Duke, a physician who talked me through a trip to the hospital.

A big tip for the folks at Joe's Pancake House for serving *juevos rancheros* on Planet Up & At 'em. And to Nancy in Alaska for going all out to restore Mandy to Over-the-Moon.

Many thanks to Gary Belair for opening his life to legend. And to Andy V. for his invitation to read before a generous audience in Erie, Pa.

To my sister Karen for picking up Tobias Wolff's book *Old School* that kept me pacified while riding east to west. And to Jane Anderson for inviting Rufus into my life.

To Mike & Barbara, Thasia & Bear, Rich, Chuck, Mark, George...and all the poets trudging toward Valhalla as a younger wave sweeps in.

To Douglas and to Jackie for the courage of their work, and to Sharon for her generous support during a rough patch.

Un gran abrazo for my cousin John who confines his sorrow to following his own nose.

Note: My decision to stop at 80 pieces coincided with the fact I was reading W. Somerset Maugham's *The Painted Veil* (1925) which alas, also stopped at Chapter 80.

Quotations borrowed from:

- *Bread for the Journey,* Henri J.M. Nouwen, New York: HarperCollins, 1997.

- *Journey into the Whirlwind,* Eugenia Semyonovna Ginzburg, New York: Harcourt, Inc.,1967.

- *The One Inside*, Sam Shepard, New York: Knopf, 2018.

- Amma Syncletica quote from *The Cloister Walk*, Kathleen Norris, New York: Riverhead Books, 1996.

- *Ahead of All Parting: The Selected Poetry and Prose off Ranier Maria Rilke*, Stephen Mitchell, trans. New York: Modern Library, 1995.

- *Listen to the Desert*, Gregory Mayer, Liguoti, MO: Liguori/Triumph, 1996.

- *Gilda* (1946), Chas. Vidor, dir., screenplay: Jo Eisinger, Ben Hecht (uncredited), featuring Rita Hayworth, Glenn Ford, George Macready, Joseph Calleia. Columbia Pictures.

- *The Band Wagon* (1953), Vincent Minnelli, dir., screenplay: Comden & Green, Alan Jay Learner; starring Fred Astaire, Cyd Charisse, Oscar Levant. Metro-Goldwyn Mayer.

About the Author

Peterson grew up in western Pa. and went to school all over. He studied his craft under the tutelage of author Georges Agadjanian, poet James. J. McAuley and novelist John Keeble. In 2003 he founded, with artist Sharon Dolan, the Actors' Mission in Rock Springs, WY. Over thirty volumes of poems and stories comprise his life's work entitled *The Literature of Missing Persons*. Peterson taught for twenty-five seasons. During that time he raised two daughters and bought a house. He resides in the Southwest and travels sparingly.

Printed in the United States
by Baker & Taylor Publisher Services